INNOVATORS FEEDING THE PLANET

Robyn Hardyman

LUCENT
PRESS

Published in 2020 by
Lucent Press, an Imprint of Greenhaven Publishing, LLC
353 3rd Avenue
Suite 255
New York, NY 10010

Produced for Lucent by Calcium
Designers: Paul Myerscough and Simon Borrough
Picture researcher: Rachel Blount
Editors: Sarah Eason and Jennifer Sanderson

Picture credits: Cover: Shutterstock: FeelGoodLuck; Inside: Beladon: p. 35; Brooklyn Grange Rooftop Farm: pp. 1r, 36, 37; Greenwave: p. 43; Plenty Unlimited Inc.: p. 34; Sanku: pp. 30, 31; Seeds&Chips, the Global Food Innovation Summit: p. 7; Shutterstock: AJP: pp. 3, 11; Allgord: p. 20; Anyaivanova: p. 10; Marcin Balcerzak: p. 6; Stephane Bidouze: p. 45; Mark Brandon: p. 44; Rich Carey: p. 38; Dainty_Picture: p. 29; Jason Finn: p. 41; Foto-Sabine: p. 40; Globe Guide Media Inc: p. 33; Brent Hofacker: p. 27; Adriana Iacob: p. 18; Patrick Jennings: p. 26; Anjo Kan: p. 15; Tomasz Klejdysz: p. 12; Andrzej Kubik: p. 19; Natalia Kuzmina: p. 4; Adriana Mahdalova: p. 16; Pete Niesen: pp. 1cl, 42; Pecold: p. 14; Andre Silva Pinto: pp. 22, 23; Sima: p. 17; Stanislav71: p. 21; The Art of Brani: p. 5; PENG TIANLI: p. 32; Suttirat Wiriyanon: p. 28; Ken Wolter: p. 13; SmartCatch: p. 39; SweetPot/Subject Capture Photography: pp. 24-25; Thought For Food/Jelmer de Haas: pp. 1l, 8, 9.

Cataloging-in-Publication Data

Names: Hardyman, Robyn.
Title: Innovators feeding the planet / Robyn Hardyman.
Description: New York : Lucent Press, 2020. | Series: Earth's innovators | Includes glossary and index.
Identifiers: ISBN 9781534565548 (pbk.) | ISBN 9781534565555 (library bound) | ISBN 9781534565562 (ebook)
Subjects: LCSH: Hunger--Juvenile literature. | Hunger--Prevention--Juvenile literature. | Food relief-- Juvenile literature. | Agricultural assistance--Juvenile literature.
Classification: LCC HV696.F6 H37 2020 | DDC 363.8'5--dc23

Printed in the United States of America

CPSIA compliance information: Batch #BS19KL:
For further information, contact Greenhaven Publishing, LLC, New York, New York, at 1-844-317-7404.

Please visit our website, www.greenhavenpublishing.com.
For a free color catalog of all our high-quality books, call toll free 1-844-317-7404 or fax 1-844-317-7405.

Contents

CHAPTER 1

A TRULY GLOBAL CHALLENGE

Food and water are the most basic needs we have for survival. In the modern world, our technology has allowed us to develop systems for feeding billions of people, yet still our need for food is creating major challenges in several ways. Innovators around the world are working on solutions to these challenges in projects of every size and kind.

Too Much and Too Little

There are more than 7.6 billion people in the world today. Billions of them do not have enough to eat, and every day many people die from malnutrition and hunger. On the other hand, in the most developed parts of the world, billions of people are eating far too much and are overweight. They are eating too much of the wrong kinds of food, and not enough of the healthier kinds. Obesity is leading to diseases that cause major problems for our health care systems.

This corn farm in Iowa is typical of the enormous scale of modern agriculture in the wealthiest areas of the world.

By the year 2050, it is predicted that the world's population could be about 9.8 billion. This would require about 70 percent more food than we consume today. Already our systems of food production are causing harm to the planet, because we are using its resources wastefully and polluting the soil, the water, and the atmosphere. Our agriculture needs to be more sustainable to save the environment, more productive to feed a growing population, and more balanced to share the food we produce more fairly around the world.

Working Together

Agriculture is an important industry. Millions of people's lives depend on the money made from growing food. Feeding the world sustainably and effectively needs to provide livelihoods for farmers as well as nutritious food for those who eat it. Individuals in their local communities, scientists in their labs, businesses, and governments are all contributing their knowledge, creativity, and energy to provide solutions to the problem. The World Economic Forum (WEF) is a nonprofit international organization committed to improving the state of the world by engaging leaders in business, government, and other areas to work together. It has set up a global project called the System Initiative on Shaping the Future of Food. This is to support innovation and the communication of ideas, and to encourage leaders and experts to work together.

In some areas of the world, the desert is advancing across land that was once suitable for growing food.

Innovators Around the World

To meet the challenge of feeding the world, innovators are looking at a range of solutions. Many are using the latest science and technology, with new developments coming through all the time. Scientific and technological innovation can take many forms. Some innovation uses the power of the Internet for improving communication in the chains of food production; other innovation uses cutting-edge science to develop new technologies for growing our food.

Connecting Innovators

The Internet has created a world that is more connected than ever before. When you are trying to launch a new idea, that connectedness can be fantastic. Barnraiser is a U.S. company that helps food innovators and entrepreneurs raise money for their projects through crowdfunding. Crowdfunding is when many people hear about a project online and each gives a small amount of money to support it. The result is an amount large enough to fund the project's development. Barnraiser is a great success story that has raised more than $1 billion for food innovators so far.

Scientists are working on new technologies for growing crops, to make them produce higher yields while using fewer resources such as water and fertilizer.

nnovation #FoodTech #AgTech #WaterFirst

rnetOfFood #ClimateChange #

SEEDS & CHIP

Innovators from around the world share their ideas at the Global Food Innovation Summit every year.

Supporting Innovators

Another organization, called EAT, manages a global community of scientists and businesses who aim to transform our food system. It was founded by a Norwegian scientist, Dr. Gunhild A. Stordalen, who encourages partnerships between experts in science and business, as well as trying to influence politicians around the world. EAT has become a powerful and effective force for change.

Seeds & Chips is another effective organization supporting change. Every year, it hosts the Global Food Innovation Summit to showcase national and international talent from science and business. The summit also features the latest cutting-edge solutions to the problems of feeding the world in a sustainable way.

INGENIOUS INNOVATIONS

There are many small projects underway around the world to address the challenge of feeding the world well. To support them and to help them share ideas, there needs to be a hub, a central, coordinating place. An organization in the United States called Food+TechConnect does just that. Since 2010 it has brought food innovators together both online and at events, and given them technical and business advice and training. People who would never normally get together, such as farmers, investors, chefs, journalists, entrepreneurs, and technologists, can collaborate and explore their ideas for the future of the food industry.

7

Thought For Food

Christine Gould grew up in the United States and studied science and technology policy at Columbia University in New York. Gould cares passionately about the problem of feeding the world. She recognized that this big challenge is likely to have the greatest impact on the lives of today's young people, who will live to see its consequences if we do not act to change our ways. It is their future that is at stake. That is why Gould decided to bring young people together to share their energy and creativity in thinking about long-term solutions. In 2012, she set up Thought For Food, a powerful community of science and technology students from top universities around the world who are working on bold, breakthrough solutions to the challenge of feeding the world.

Participants at the 2018 Thought For Food Academy learned about the challenges that farmers face today.

These 2018 participants worked on the important topic of planting more trees in urban areas, gardens, streets, and parks.

Young-People Power

Today, Thought For Food includes more than 12,000 young innovators in 160 countries around the world. Gould says there are six attitudes that these young people share. These are the things that drive them and make them so brilliant at what they do. They are: being open to new ideas, being willing to collaborate with others, having a lot of curiosity about the world, not being afraid to fail before they succeed, wanting to make a difference in people's lives, and having a lot of energy. She believes that, with these qualities, everyone has the potential to make a difference. If they can come together and collaborate, there is so much these young people can do.

Coming Together

Each year, Thought For Food holds a global competition where promising ideas are launched. The ten finalists in the competition present their projects at the Thought For Food Summit, a large event where these young innovators come together to share their ideas and gain inspiration from each other. In 2018, these teams came from Australia, Brazil, Ghana, Jordan, Kenya, Malaysia, Nigeria, the United Kingdom (U.K.), and the United States. Their ideas ranged from helping farmers to dry their grains more effectively to increasing the sustainability of fertilizers, and improving the quality of water in poor regions. Since the Thought For Food Challenge was launched in 2013, more than 40 new ventures have been started around the world, putting exciting new ideas into everyday action, to really make a difference.

CHAPTER 2

GROWING MORE

Our planet has only a limited amount of land available for growing food. Much of the world's land is covered by oceans or by mountains, or is too wet or too dry. This means we must use all our energy and creativity to find new ways to grow more food with the resources we have.

Staple Foods

The five biggest crops grown in the world are corn, wheat, rice, potatoes, and cassava. Corn is a staple food in much of Africa, while rice is a staple in Asia. Wheat covers more of Earth than any other crop, while cassava is important in Africa and South America. Other crops grown in huge quantities are the cereal sorghum, soybeans, and sweet potatoes.

Scientists are constantly looking at new ways to grow more food.

Rice farmers in India use traditional methods to dry their crops, but a significant amount of the rice is lost to rot.

Modifying Genes

To grow more of these foods, innovators have looked at ways of developing new varieties of them that will produce a higher yield and therefore, more food. The new varieties may be more resistant to drought or need less fertilizer or water to grow. These new varieties are often genetically modified (GM). In GM food, the genes of the plant, which define its characteristics, are altered. New genes may be added from different plants, to give the new plant the characteristics that famers want it to have.

Some people are cautious about GM crops in case there is a harmful effect on the environments in which they grow. This could happen if they cross-pollinate with existing varieties of plants and crops. Some people worry that increase in yields may make more money for large-scale farmers in the West, but not for small-scale farmers in developing countries.

INGENIOUS INNOVATIONS

One important way to increase the yield from crops is to dry them properly after they are harvested. The equipment to do this effectively can be too expensive for farmers in poorer countries. They use traditional methods instead, which waste about 30 percent of the crop. One innovation from a group based in Malaysia and the U.K. is SunRice. This is a free drying service that travels from one farmer to another. The rice is dried in a solar-powered dryer called the solar bubble. About 30 percent more usable rice is produced this way, and it is of a higher quality. SunRice buys the rice from the farmer and sells it on. The farmer makes more money because their crop is bigger and better, and SunRice makes money to invest in more solar bubbles for more small farmers.

11

Pests and Waste

Farmers growing crops face two enormous challenges. The first is pests. These can attack a healthy crop, wiping out a farmer's income and destroying valuable food. The other challenge comes from waste because harvested crops go bad. This happens faster in hot climates than in cool ones, but large-scale producers use techniques such as refrigeration to delay it. In developing countries, refrigeration may not be available.

The main way that farmers protect against pests is by using chemicals called pesticides. These are expensive and can also be harmful to the environment. Farmers in poorer areas have fewer defenses against pests. Some new varieties of crop, however, have been engineered with built-in protection against pests. One GM potato variety, for example, needs 80 percent less pesticide than other kinds.

The wheat weevil beetle is a major pest for farmers of wheat crops everywhere.

The Old and the New

Concerns about genetic engineering have led innovators to look for other ways to combat pests. One is amazingly simple: to mix very old varieties from remote areas with modern new ones. For example, in the United States Midwest, the hotter summers in recent years have brought devastating attacks on farmers' wheat crops by a pest called the Hessian fly. Yields have fallen by 10 percent. However, scientists discovered that wheat-related grasses that grow wild in Syria in the Middle East have a natural resistance to Hessian fly, developed over thousands of years in that hot climate. In fact, the grasses are resistant to many other pests, too. Now they are working on combining the two into a new wheat variety, with better pest protection.

A family-owned business based in Switzerland, called Vestergaard, has developed a different kind of protection against pests. Vestergaard's scientific research has resulted in a product called the ZeroFly Storage Bag. This is a bag to hold the farmer's seeds before sowing or the grain after harvest, and it is made using fibers covered in insecticide. This prevents the contents being infested and destroyed by beetles and weevils. With this simple solution, farmers can safely store their harvest and wait to sell it until prices are favorable.

What a Waste

One innovator in Nigeria has come up with a solution to extend the life of perishable foods. Coating+ is a safe, edible coating for plants and vegetables that is added as soon as they are harvested. It slows down the process of the food rotting and it also preserves the nutrient quality of the foods, allowing them to be stored for longer.

Farmers in the Midwest are looking at using a mix of old and new varieties to make their wheat crops more resistant to pests.

Wakati

According to data produced by the United Nations (UN), 45 percent of all the fruit and vegetables that farmers in developing countries grow is wasted before their products reach the market. This is a terrible waste of valuable food. It also affects the incomes that these farmers can earn, and because many of them are living in poverty, they really need as much income as possible. One innovative group of scientists in Belgium—made up of Arne Pauwels, Arno Nurski, and Michael Gykiere—developed a product to help these farmers reduce the waste of their crops. This is the Wakati.

No Refrigeration

Temperatures in developing countries are often high. In these conditions, foods rot much more quickly after harvest because they start to lose water. However, as there is often little or no electricity, there is no way to run refrigerators to slow down this process and keep the foods fresher for longer. Like so many of the best ideas, the Wakati looks very simple. It is a special tent, made of airtight fabric, which creates a damp, humid environment to prevent this dehydration from happening.

This farmer in Uganda, Africa, depends on her crops for income, but they begin to rot soon after they are harvested, so the selling period is very short.

These Ugandan farmers sell their tomatoes along the road as soon as they are harvested. With Wakati, they could keep them for longer to get a better price.

A Simple Idea

To do this, Wakati needs a little power and some water. The power comes from the sun. A small solar-powered unit provides enough electricity to run the device inside the tent. The device holds 0.25 gallons (1 l) of water and makes it evaporate slowly over time, creating damp conditions. One simple, pop-up Wakati tent can store up to 440 pounds (200 kg) of crops at a time.

From the beginning, the Belgian scientists tested Wakati with real growers in challenging locations in Uganda in East Africa, Afghanistan in Asia, and Haiti in the Caribbean.

In Uganda, Anna Icumar and her husband grow oranges, tomatoes, and mangoes. When these are harvested, they must take them straight to the market before they begin to rot. When they were testing the Wakati, they stored their produce on the farm instead, where it remained in good condition. When they did choose to sell it, they got a better price because it looked healthy and because they could choose the best time to sell, when demand for the fruit was high.

Wakati could be used farther down the supply chain in these countries, at collection points for produce from many farms to transport to cities.

CHAPTER 3

IMPROVING THE LAND

For crops to grow well, the soil needs to be rich in nutrients and to have a good supply of water. In some parts of the world, getting these conditions can be a challenge. The soil becomes poor in quality from growing the same crops over and over, yet commercially produced, artificial fertilizer is expensive and, over time, it damages the soil.

Expensive Fertilizer

Feeding crops in the developing world is a challenge. Fertilizer is expensive and the farmer may not know how much to use or when is the best time to use it. One innovative project based in Australia is RiceHarvest. It was started by engineering student Joseph Shen, who is working with rice farmers in Burma in Southeast Asia. Shen and his team bring digital technology to the problem in the form of an app. The farmer downloads the app and photographs 10 leaves in their field. The app uses the color of the leaves to diagnose how much fertilizer is needed and recommend when to apply it. Later, the farmer records the yield so that even better recommendations can be given for the next harvest. The farmer is keeping costs to a minimum, while improving their income from a higher yield.

Small farms like this one in Kenya are using the Safi Sarvi fertilizer to increase the yields from their crops.

Soybeans coated with the microbes that protect them from disease produce a higher yield, without using more water or fertilizer.

Another project improving farmers' yields and incomes through fertilizer is Safi Sarvi. It was founded by Riley Rodgers and Kevin Kung in the United States and Samuel Rigu in Kenya to provide high-quality, locally available fertilizer to small-scale farmers in Kenya. Commercially produced fertilizers are not only expensive, but they also harm the soil over time. The Safi Sarvi product makes the soil more fertile and is made locally using farm waste in a process developed by Rodgers and Kung. Farmers using it have seen their incomes double as yields rise and their costs fall.

Improved Seeds

Indigo Agriculture is another innovator in this field. Started by David Perry in Boston, Massachusetts, it cultivates the beneficial microbes that are found naturally in plants and that have traditionally protected the plants from diseases. The chemicals in modern farming methods have greatly reduced the presence of these microbes, so Indigo has found a way to bring them back, not in the form of a fertilizer but by coating the crop's seeds with them before they are planted. Crops grown from these seeds produce yields about 15 percent higher, without any extra fertilizer or water. So far, Indigo has launched enhanced seeds for five major crops: corn, cotton, rice, soybeans, and wheat.

Holding Back the Desert

In some developing countries, one big challenge for farmers is to prevent their land becoming poorer in quality, and therefore not suitable for growing crops or supporting animals. Several factors can cause this process, known as desertification. The land may be eroded by the wind or by water, or it may lose nutrients through the overuse of chemicals and bad management, such as growing the same crops over and over. In Africa, the Caribbean, Asia, Latin America, and the Pacific, individuals and organizations are working to stop this process, which causes hunger and poverty.

Fighting Desertification

Supported by the UN, Action Against Desertification is working in the Caribbean, the Pacific, and Africa. In Africa, the focus is the Great Green Wall program, which aims to improve the land near the continent's largest desert, the Sahara, planting a wide belt of trees and bushes that can protect the agricultural land from the advance of the sand. This is a huge project that will take many years.

Desertification can be a problem anywhere. In Spain, people have planted native shrubs on this abandoned farmland to hold down the soil and prevent it from being eroded.

Tunisian Success

One major cause of desertification is cutting down trees. Without the tree roots to hold the soil in place, the soil is washed away by the rain or blown away by the wind. One young innovator, Sarah Toumi, decided to do something about this problem. Sarah grew up in France but visited her father's home country of Tunisia in North Africa, and saw how desertification was making local farmers poorer and poorer. She saw that farming practices needed to change, with new crops and better land management.

In 2012, Sarah moved to Tunisia and founded Acacias for All, to spread the use of acacia trees as a barrier against the growing desert. Acacias have long roots that bring to the surface essential nitrogen and fresh water. Today she shows farmers how to use 20 different kinds of trees, as well as vegetables and medicinal plants. These not only keep the soil healthy, but they provide a better income for the farmers. Sarah has overseen the planting of about 1 million trees, restoring a wide area of land to fertility. She plans to extend her program to Algeria and Morocco. In 2016, she was awarded a Rolex Award for Enterprise for her dedication to her pioneering work.

Acacia trees are proving to be a successful barrier against desertification in Tunisia, thanks to Acacias for All.

Water

All living things need water to grow. Yet in some areas of the world, water is in very short supply. The increase in temperatures around the world has made water shortages a very real problem in many countries. This impacts on their ability to grow food and their peace, because conflicts over access to water are an increasing problem.

Catching the Rain

In Guatemala, an exciting project harnesses water to improve the supply of food. One area of eastern Guatemala is very dry and farmers there struggle to produce their own food. A project devised by the Food and Agriculture Organization of the UN and funded by the Swedish government has changed everything.

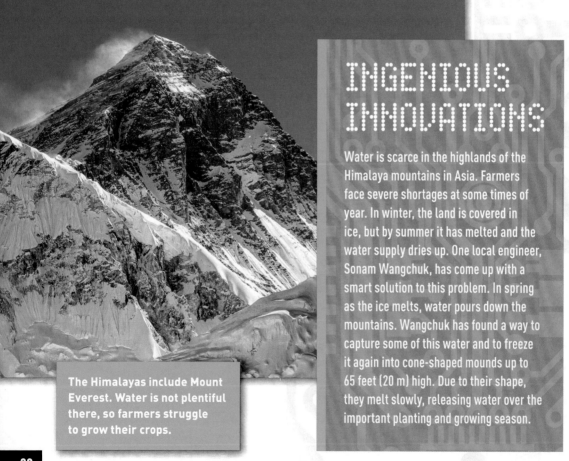

The Himalayas include Mount Everest. Water is not plentiful there, so farmers struggle to grow their crops.

INGENIOUS INNOVATIONS

Water is scarce in the highlands of the Himalaya mountains in Asia. Farmers face severe shortages at some times of year. In winter, the land is covered in ice, but by summer it has melted and the water supply dries up. One local engineer, Sonam Wangchuk, has come up with a smart solution to this problem. In spring as the ice melts, water pours down the mountains. Wangchuk has found a way to capture some of this water and to freeze it again into cone-shaped mounds up to 65 feet (20 m) high. Due to their shape, they melt slowly, releasing water over the important planting and growing season.

The simple idea is to create community reservoirs that capture what little rain there is each year, and keep it from evaporating.

These small reservoirs have made a big difference. The local people are using the water to grow more fruit and vegetables. The biggest change, however, is that they are also now cultivating fish and snails in them. They never used to eat fish, but now this valuable source of protein has been added to their diet.

This desalination plant in Dubai, in the United Arab Emirates, makes drinking water from the sea, but it is an expensive process that uses a lot of energy.

Over 200 families have their own small tanks, while larger community ones benefit 1,000 more families. Knowledge of the project is spreading in the region, bringing food and money to more of the world's poorest people.

Using the Ocean

The oceans are full of water, but salt water cannot be used for growing food. Desalination is an expensive process, but one young innovator from the University of Victoria in Australia, Devesh Bharadwaj, has found a way of reducing the energy needed to do it by up to 30 percent. His company, Pani Energy, is working with desalination plants in Europe, Africa, and Australia to advance this technology.

SOLHO

The challenge of increasing our food production while using fewer resources is particularly high in regions of the world that have little water and low levels of development. What these areas often do have, however, is a lot of sunshine. One innovator is using this advantage to help them grow more food.

Using the Sun

SOLHO is a company set up by Adriano Desideri and Emiliano Casati, researchers at Delft University of Technology in the Netherlands. SOLHO uses solar power, seawater, and sewage to provide the resources needed to run greenhouses that are growing food. They call their system the Solar-Powered Horticultural Off-Grid Unit, or SPRHOUT.

Farmers like this one in Angola, Africa, could grow more crops in a greenhouse without using electricity.

SPRHOUT uses solar power, so it can be used to power greenhouses in remote areas. The system uses special panels to collect solar energy in the form of heat. The heat energy is then used to generate the right amount of heating or cooling needed for growing plants in the greenhouse. It also takes in either seawater or wastewater, which it converts into the clean water that is essential for growing the crops.

This innovative system has many benefits. It can operate 24 hours a day, and it can even be operated remotely, from a distance, without trained operators. This saves the farmer costs. The system uses only the power of the sun, so it does not produce any harmful emissions to pollute Earth's atmosphere. SPRHOUT can also work on a small or a large scale, and be scaled up or down in size to meet the needs of individual growers.

SPRHOUT provides an answer to the problems of energy and of water surrounding food production that many growers around the world are facing today. SPRHOUT's inventors are very proud of their achievement and it has also won several prestigious awards. In 2017, it was one of four winners in the European Union (E.U.) Top 50 Millennial Start-Ups Competition. In April 2018, it was chosen as the winner in the category "Energy, Water and Food" at the Start-Up Energy Transition Awards.

With a greenhouse powered by **SPRHOUT**, farmers can water their crops using seawater or wastewater, which the unit cleans. They do not have to walk through their fields, watering them by hand with freshwater, as this Angolan farmer is doing in a very time-consuming process.

CHAPTER 4

IMPROVING NUTRITION

As well as growing more food, we need to grow better food, food that is more nutritious, to improve the quality of the diet of people around the world. This is especially important in the poorest areas of the world, where food is in short supply and eating a healthy, balanced diet is difficult for millions of people. Innovators have set their sights on addressing this challenge.

Improved Rice

One important way to improve people's diet, and therefore their health, is to enhance the nutrition in existing foods. Rice is the staple food for billions of people in Asia, and one company, DSM, is developing rice grains with a higher nutritional value than ordinary rice. Rice kernels are ground into rice flour, fortified, or enriched, with extra vitamins and minerals, then formed back into rice grains. The resulting product is called NutriRice, and studies have shown that it can significantly improve people's nutrition. Children who eat NutriRice regularly are physically in better shape, and they are better able to concentrate at school.

Sweetpot

A team of innovators in Ghana, West Africa, is developing an enhanced product to solve the problem of vitamin A deficiency, which can cause blindness and even death. The team includes Maame Ekua Manful from France and Ewura-Esi Manful and Raphael Aidoo from the Kwame Nikumah University of Science and Technology in Ghana.

The team has created Sweetpot, a yogurt that has vitamin A and dietary fiber added to it. After milk, yogurt is the second most popular dairy product in Ghana. The extra vitamin A in this new product comes from adding sweet potatoes, which are widely grown locally.

There are many advantages to Sweetpot. Sweet potatoes are a cheaper source of vitamin A than artificial versions, and they are plentiful locally. They are naturally sweet so no added sugar is necessary. They also provide extra fiber, which is important for a healthy diet. This makes the yogurt thicker and therefore more filling, making people feel less hungry. Finally, the farmers who grow sweet potatoes have a new market for their produce, so their incomes grow, too.

Sweetpot yogurt has been developed as a simple but effective way to improve the nutrition of people in Ghana.

The Problem with Meat

In the developed world, we eat a lot of meat. We love food like chicken, burgers, and steaks. The problem with this is that farming meat is very intensive. That means it uses a lot of natural resources, such as land, water, and crops. It is also bad for the environment, producing substances that contribute to global warming and climate change.

In the past 50 years, meat consumption has risen fourfold. With the world's population rising, and more people able to afford to buy and eat meat as they become wealthier, our level of meat consumption is not sustainable. The United States alone consumes 26 billion pounds (12 billion kg) of beef each year. One cow can consume 11,000 gallons (42,000 l) of water a year. We need to find new ways to feed our habit for meat. As Bill Gates said in 2013, "There is no way to produce enough meat for 9 billion people."

Raising cattle uses huge amounts of water and land, and produces harmful emissions that are polluting our planet.

Lab Meat

Scientists have been experimenting with new techniques for "growing" meat. They have used special cells from animals, called stem cells, to grow new muscle tissue in the laboratory. This lab-grown meat could one day become more efficient to produce than traditional beef, lamb, pork, and chicken. One company in the United States, called Finless, is also looking at growing lab fish in this way. At the moment, it is still too expensive to produce to make it a realistic alternative, but the technology is advancing all the time.

Fake Meat

Maybe we are not going to be eating lab-grown burgers any time soon, but another alternative to natural meat is coming along much more quickly. This is meat substitutes, or fake meat products that look, feel, and taste like the real thing. Innovative companies and investors are taking this technology very seriously. One Californian company, Beyond Meat, created a burger that is made entirely from plant-based ingredients. It is made mostly from vegetable protein found in peas. The meaty color comes from using beets, and the juiciness comes from coconut oil and potato starch. Beyond Meat was founded by Ethan Brown and backed by Bill Gates. Other companies are innovating along the same lines.

The Impossible Burger is now also widely available, and businesses across the developed world are creating more meat-free, nutrition-rich, meaty treats.

Meat-free, plant-based burgers are a delicious, healthy, and planet-friendly alternative to the burgers we consume by the millions.

New Foods

We have seen how plants can be used to create protein-rich foods that look, taste, and feel like meat. Of course these plants can also be used to create other kinds of new food. Innovators are working on these, and on developing other kinds of new food, to help feed the world.

Bug Steak?

Meat is a good source of the protein that our bodies need, but there is another source of protein that is much, much more plentiful in the world—bugs. In many parts of the world, eating insects is already common. Deep-fried locusts are widely eaten in Southeast Asia, and yellow jacket larvae are popular in Japan, for example. The trend is spreading, but in developed countries it is still small. One young U.S. innovator, Harman Singh Johar, wants to change all that. He is intent on turning crickets, grasshoppers, and other insects into staples of the U.S. diet, and a solution to malnutrition worldwide. Johar founded an insect supply business, World Ento, at 19, and now advises governments on the power of projects like his to feed the world. His company, Aspire, farms and processes about 5 million crickets each week.

Grasshoppers, silkworms, crickets, and locusts are regularly served up as street food in Thailand and other Southeast Asian countries.

Little-Known Fruit

Some little-known foods that are very nutritious could be grown much more widely to feed more people. In Ethiopia, East Africa, for example, there is an ancient fruit called the enset. It looks a bit like a banana and it can feed more people per square foot of crop than most cereals. Enset can be made into three main foods—kocho, bulla, and amicho. The pulp of the roots and leaves is fermented underground for several months to make kocho, which is used in dough to make bread. Bulla is harvested from fully matured plants, and is used in soups and porridges; it can even be used to make pancakes. Amicho is the boiled root, and is similar to the potato. Enset is resistant to bad weather, which is why it is known locally as "the tree against hunger." Scientists are working on ways to grow this amazing crop in new places.

INGENIOUS INNOVATIONS

Another interesting new source of protein is the seeds of a plant called the sweet blue lupine. German scientist Stephanie Mittermaier has developed a process to extract the protein from the seeds of this legume plant, which grows in many different climates, even in sandy and other poor soils. The resulting protein tastes like dairy products. Lupinesse ice cream is today widely available across Germany, and this technology could be used in developing countries where dairy protein is not widely available.

The seeds of the sweet blue lupine are an excellent source of protein.

Sanku

Felix Brooks-Church is a U.S. innovator and entrepreneur who has lived and worked across six developing countries. On his travels, he has seen for himself the difference that good nutrition brings to people's lives. When people eat a better diet, they are sick less often and are able to go to school or to work. While Brooks-Church was touring hundreds of grain mills in at-risk communities across South Asia and East and Southern Africa, he became determined to do something to improve the quality of local people's food.

Adding Nutrition

Brooks-Church cofounded Sanku, a nonprofit company working on fortifying flour with the essential vitamins and minerals we all need in our diet. These extra nutrients include iron, folic acid, zinc, and vitamin B12. They are added at the small mills where the harvested grains are processed and turned into fortified flour. Everything that is made with that flour therefore has a better nutritional value.

Sanku works at the local level. Most people who live in remote rural areas of developing countries eat foods produced very close to their homes.

Felix Brooks-Church of Sanku is at work in this African flour mill.

Sanku works with local millers to make their flour more nutritious without adding to its cost.

They need a small-scale solution to improving the nutrition in the foods they eat. Sanku's game-changing product is a dosifier, a device that automatically and precisely adds the essential vitamins and minerals to the flour at small, local flour mills in Africa.

Flour Bags

How does the local miller afford the cost of the nutrients? It is a neat solution. Sanku buys empty flour bags in huge quantities, so they get them more cheaply than the miller could. They sell these empty flour bags to the miller for a lower price than they would pay elsewhere.

The money they save pays for the nutrients to go in the flour. So the miller's costs have not risen, but their flour is fortified with goodness. Sanku monitors the miller's use of the dosifier remotely using cell phones, and pays regular visits to check that all is going well.

The Sanku dosifier technology is installed across five countries in East and Southern Africa: Tanzania, Rwanda, Kenya, Malawi, and Mozambique. This success story is nourishing up to 1 million of the world's most vulnerable people. By 2021, Sanku is aiming to have 3,000 mills in operation, feeding up to 20 million people.

CHAPTER 5

URBAN FOODS

By 2025, around 70 percent of the world's population will be living in cities, up from 55 percent in 2018. If we are going to keep all these city-dwellers well fed, it makes sense to move some of our food production closer to where they live. There are some exciting technological developments making this possible in cities around the world.

Planted in Air

Plants need water and nutrients to grow and, although they usually get these from the soil, they can be grown in other ways. Hydroponics is the process of growing plants in water with added nutrients, but no soil. Aeroponics is the process of growing plants in an air or mist environment, without the use of soil or water. In a time when the water supply is under pressure in many areas, these new technologies have a huge benefit. Aeroponics uses 95 percent less water than farming in fields, and 40 percent less water than hydroponics.

These strawberries are growing indoors using hydroponics. They grow at heights that make them easier for people to pick than traditional growing methods.

At this aeroponics farm, the plants do not grow in either soil or water. They are watered and fed using a mist-spraying system.

Both these systems operate indoors, in carefully controlled environments. There are no challenges from the weather or from pests, and the "farms" can be in multistory buildings in the heart of cities. Light levels are carefully controlled with low-energy lights, and the nutrients in the water or the mist are designed to make the crops grow fast and taste great. The temperature is carefully controlled, too.

High-Rise Farming

Singapore in Asia is one of the most densely populated nations in the world, with little land available for farming. Here, one inventor and entrepreneur, Jack Ng, created a system he calls Sky Greens, to grow more food in less space, but still using natural light. It is like a plant skyscraper. A collection of 32 trays of greens, such as lettuce and spinach, is arranged on a tall, narrow A-frame structure. The structure slowly rotates, like a Ferris wheel, so that each tray gets enough exposure to sunlight. Sky Greens began operating commercially a few years ago, and now delivers fresh vegetables to the markets of Singapore every day. This innovative idea makes minimal use of land, water, and energy resources, and is sure to spread to more cities around the world.

Grown on Your Doorstep

Innovative projects to bring the creation of food closer to the people who eat it are being developed all around the world.

Plenty

Plenty is a dynamic, innovative company that Matt Barnard and Nate Storey cofounded in San Francisco, California, in 2013. It has developed the technology to grow leafy greens in indoor farms. The difference is that they grow not in the ground but vertically. Towers 20 feet (6 m) high hold the crops, which grow using hydroponics and low-energy lights. There is no soil involved. This system uses less space than the vertical trays used by other hydroponic growers. Sensors adjust the light, heat, and water as needed. Plenty focuses on leafy greens and herbs, and will soon grow strawberries and tomatoes. It says it can use the system to grow anything except root vegetables and tree fruits.

On a Plenty farm, the plants grow vertically up long towers. The farm team checks their progress, but their water, light, and heat levels are all remotely controlled.

This floating farm in the Netherlands will be home to 40 cows and their milk will be processed on-site.

This kind of farming can produce much more food per square foot than land farming. Plenty is a big success story. It has attracted millions of dollars of investment and is expanding across the United States. It will soon open its first farm in the Middle East.

Keep It Local

There will always be a big place for traditional farming, of course. One innovator in the Chicago, Illinois, area is trying to modernize the way food is farmed by and delivered to local communities. FamilyFarmed, set up by Jim Slama, is working to build a better food system, one that urges everyone to eat food produced as locally as possible using sustainable and fair practices. This is the Good Food movement, developing regional, sustainable food systems that give consumers better food and producers better markets closer to farms.

INGENIOUS INNOVATIONS

The first offshore dairy farm in the world is in the busy port of Rotterdam in the Netherlands. Two innovators, Peter and Minke van Wingerden, came up with the idea to keep cows close to the consumers of their milk in the city. Their company, Beladon, built a three-story floating platform out on the water to house 40 cows that live in a garden-like environment and are milked by robots. The milk is processed right there and turned into dairy products. The waste the cows produce is turned into natural fertilizer on-site, too. Visitors can see the cows and learn more about the processes. The project is starting small, but has huge potential to be scaled up in cities beside the water all over the world.

Brooklyn Grange

The city of New York may be just about the last place you would expect to find food being farmed. It is one of the busiest cities in the world, with high-rise buildings as far as the eye can see. Yet this dynamic place is the location for Brooklyn Grange, and it is growing high-quality nutritious food for local people.

Sky High

Brooklyn Grange is the leading rooftop farming and intensive green roofing business in the United States. It is the innovative idea of Ben Flanner, Anastasia Cole Plakias, and Gwen Schantz. All three of these people left their desk jobs to start the business because they believe in bringing healthy, delicious vegetables to people living in urban areas, while doing the environment some good at the same time. Brooklyn Grange now operates the world's largest rooftop soil farms, with more than 247,000 square feet (5.6 acres) in cultivation in the Brooklyn and Queens boroughs of the city. They have grown and sold more than 500,000 pounds (227,000 kg) of vegetables. They sell directly to restaurants, but also directly to the public at weekly farmers markets.

Brooklyn Grange farms are feeding local people with the absolute minimum of "food miles" traveled.

With the New York City skyline in the distance, farmers work on growing a wide variety of healthy foods for local people.

Three Innovators

Each of the three young innovators plays a significant role in the project. Ben Flanner is the one in charge of the agricultural side of the operation, choosing the crops and managing their growth through the year, while Anastasia Cole Plakias looks after sales, marketing, and communications aspects of the business. Gwen Schantz is in charge of the design and building of the farms. She also looks for other available places in the city to create growing spaces wherever she can. All three are passionate about their work and eager to spread their message about local food for local people.

Recently, Brooklyn Grange has expanded beyond its original mission to grow vegetables. It now also has egg-laying hens, and they keep bees in more than 30 naturally managed honeybee hives, on roofs across the city of New York.

Pass It On

To promote their work, Brooklyn Grange holds tours and workshops for visitors to learn about producing food this way. It also hosts magnificent dinners up on the roof, where people can enjoy delicious meals made with the food and share the good news about this innovative way of bringing great food to the city.

CHAPTER 6

FOOD FROM THE OCEAN

Around the world, about 3 billion people rely on fish as the main source of protein in their diet. Many of them live in developing countries, and without fish they would not be properly nourished. However, we have been taking fish out of the rivers and oceans at such a high rate for decades that our fish stocks are now under severe pressure.

Bycatch

We are taking too many fish out of the ocean. The UN noted in its 2016 report "The State of World Fisheries and Aquaculture" that nearly one-third of wild fish stocks are overfished, and more than half are being fully fished. Part of the problem lies with the techniques used by many commercial fishers. They simply drag huge nets through the water, and haul in whatever gets caught in them. Many of these will be fish species they do not want or cannot sell but once they have been caught, they die. They are thrown back into the water, dead. This is called bycatch.

Traditional fishing methods have caught far too many tuna at one time in huge nets.

INGENIOUS INNOVATIONS

Rob Terry has set up SmartCatch, a sustainable seafood technology company to help fishers catch only the fish that they want, with less bycatch. DigiCatch is a remote-controlled computer and video system used inside fishing nets underwater. The system shows exactly what is in the net. If the fishers see too many fish that they do not want, they can release those fish before the nets are hauled in.

SmartCatch helps fishers be more careful about what they take from the ocean.

Exit This Way

Around the world, the regulations against bycatch are tightening, so fishers need help reducing it. Innovators are designing new technologies to help them with this. One young British designer named Dan Watson was studying design engineering at Glasgow University in Scotland, U.K., when he came up with his innovative idea. He created SafetyNet Technologies, which develops devices that use light to attract the intended catch and repel the species they do not want. Different sea species respond to light in different ways, depending on the wavelength or how the lights flash. This makes them either swim toward or away from the nets, reducing the unintended catch.

Another innovation comes from a U.S. fisher, Christopher Brown. He fishes for squid and has designed a net that allows him to catch them with very little bycatch. His net contains an escape route at its base, so that fish species that naturally swim at greater depths, such as flounder, can flee through it.

Sharing Ideas

The World Wildlife Fund (WWF) wants to encourage more innovators to come forward to help solve this problem. It runs a regular competition called the International Smart Gear Competition, which gives researchers, conservation specialists, and fishers the chance to share their ideas. The winners receive prize money to develop their projects.

Aquaculture

Aquaculture is the breeding, rearing, and harvesting of fish and shellfish in all types of water environment. The fish and the seafood are farmed, just like animals on land. Aquaculture is big business. As the supplies of fresh fish in the wild have come under increasing pressure in recent decades, more and more businesses have started growing fish in these controlled environments.

Bright Ideas

In the United States, marine aquaculture produces many sea-dwelling species, including oysters, clams, mussels, shrimp, and seaweeds, and fish such as salmon, black sea bass, sablefish, yellowtail, and pompano. There are many ways to farm marine shellfish, including "seeding" small shellfish on the seafloor or by growing them in sinking or floating cages. Marine fish farming is typically done in net pens in the water or in tanks on land. Innovations in this area include reducing the impact of pests and diseases, making the farms more productive, and reducing any harmful effects on the environment. If fish farming is to grow to meet our need for food, it must be sustainable and efficient.

Tilapia is the third most important fish in aquaculture, after carp and salmon. These protein-rich fish are farmed in countries with tropical climates.

Fish Food

An organization called the Global Aquaculture Alliance (GAA) runs an annual Innovation Award for the best new ideas in the business. In 2017, a U.S. company called Corbion won the award. Corbion's researchers developed a feed to give to farmed salmon. The feed is made using algae (tiny plant-like creatures that grow in water), and the benefit is that it makes the fish even more nutritious. This is because it enriches their levels of omega-3 fatty acid, which we need as part of a healthy diet.

The Scottish Aquaculture Innovation Centre (SAIC) is bringing together businesses and scientists in local universities to work together on solving some of the problems of aquaculture. So far, 16 innovative projects have been supported through this collaboration. One area they are working on is the causes of disease in farmed salmon.

Aquaponics

Aquaponics takes aquaculture one step further, by combining it with hydroponics, the growing of plants in water. The two processes work together and support each other. The vegetables are fed using the waste products produced by the fish. In turn, the water the fish live in is cleaned by the growing vegetables. This amazing collaboration uses less water and prevents fish waste from being released back into the ocean. It also cuts out the need for expensive fertilizers for the plants. Ouroboros Farms is one of the largest commercial aquaponic farms in the United States. It is located in Half Moon Bay, California.

Aquaponics uses the waste products from fish to feed plants that grow in their water.

GreenWave

Bren Smith used to be a traditional commercial fisher in the United States. Working with the ocean every day, he became concerned about the rapidly falling levels of fish stocks. He was determined to do something about it, and he did—by creating GreenWave. His remarkable invention won him a $100,000 prize in the Fuller Challenge, a prize for individuals developing solutions to humanity's most pressing problems. In 2017, it was named as one of the 25 best inventions of the year by *Time* magazine. It shows what one person can do when they bring creativity and determination to a challenge.

Going Down

GreenWave supports 3D ocean farming, a system for farming vertically in the ocean close to the shore. It farms shellfish such as scallops, oysters, mussels, and clams, together with sea greens, such as kelp. They grow on vertical ropes anchored to the ocean floor. This ingenious system produces a high yield of crops, much higher than land crops over the same sized area. What is more, it does it without causing any harm to the ocean environment. In fact, it does good. The sea greens take a lot of harmful carbon out of the environment, and the shellfish absorb nitrogen. None of the crops require fertilizer, either. All they need to grow is the seawater. This is farming that fixes the environment while it feeds people.

Spread the Word

Smith's company is operating on the east coast of the United States, in New Haven, Connecticut, where Bren has helped 14 fishers set up farms. He is passionate about spreading his idea across the nation and beyond, and he makes his technology freely available to others. He gives new farmers grants, seeds, and training, and guarantees to buy their crops for five years. As he says, "Anyone with 10 acres, a boat, and $20,000 can be up and running within one year."

Foods grown this way are close to the shore, so they do not travel far to reach consumers in local restaurants. Some of the sea greens are dried and used as high-quality fertilizer for local, land-based crops. Others are turned into biofuels, which are greener alternatives to gasoline. Most, though, are welcomed by chefs and turned into delicious, nutritious dishes for diners.

Bren Smith's GreenWave grows nutritious sea greens vertically, on ropes, to produce a high yield.

INNOVATORS OF THE FUTURE

In the developed world, where farming often happens on a very large scale, new technology is leading to many new innovations. Advances that give detailed tracking and monitoring of every stage in the process of growing food are making this industrial type of farming safer, more efficient, and also more environmentally sustainable. The use of harmful fertilizers and pesticides, and of valuable resources such as water, is becoming more controlled.

Automatic Milk

One innovation on large dairy farms is a robotic milking system. These ingenious systems can recognize each animal, give it an amount of food based on its individual needs, and then milk it, all automatically. During the whole process, data is collected on each animal, to help the famer make decisions about their herd. With herds of hundreds or even thousands of cows, this saves the farmer a lot of time and money.

Robotic milking systems like this one are an efficient way to manage large dairy herds.

Small-scale farmers need help, so they can produce enough food to feed local people, while also making money to stay in business.

Feather Warmth

Another challenge facing the food industry is packaging. Many fresh foods need to be kept either warm or cool when they are being transported from the supplier to the customer. The polystyrene traditionally used to insulate food on its journey is made from plastic. Plastic is not good for the environment because it is slow to break down. Two U.K. innovators, Elena Dieckmann and Ryan Robinson, have invented a way to make a new insulation material from something that has already been used for that purpose—feathers. The product is called Pluumo, and it uses the feathers that are left over on chicken farms when the birds are processed. After use, the material breaks down naturally. Thousands of tons of feathers are produced every day around the world, so this is a truly innovative way to make use of them, to keep foods fresh, and to reduce harm to the environment.

Supporting the Poorest

Large-scale farmers are producing huge quantities of food every year, so innovations in this area are important. In the developing world, however, many farmers are working on a very small scale, to feed just their families or their local community. They may not produce enough to eat, or to sell to support their families, so any innovations that can help them grow more food are vital. New kinds of grains, new ways to make their land fertile, and new ways of sharing the advantages we have in the developed world will all help us in the quest to meet the challenge of feeding the whole world.

Glossary

aeroponics the process of growing plants in mist, without soil

aquaculture the farming of fish and shellfish

artificial made by man

biofuels fuels from a renewable source, such as plants

bycatch fish that are caught in a fisher's net unintentionally and are not sold

commercially related to or used in the buying and selling of goods and services, for making a profit

cross-pollinate when a plant is fertilized by pollen from another type of plant

desalination the process of removing salt from seawater, to make it fit to drink or to use for farming

developed countries wealthy countries where most people have good living conditions

developing countries poorer countries that are trying to build their economies and improve people's living conditions

entrepreneurs people who have an idea and start new businesses to develop it

eroded carried away by water or wind

evaporate to turn from liquid to gas

fertilizer a substance given to crops to make them grow well

fiber the bulky matter in foods that we need to keep our digestion healthy

genes the instructions in the cells of living things that control their characteristics

genetically modified (GM) referring to plants with genes that have been altered to give them characteristics that make them grow well

hydroponics the process of growing plants in water with added nutrients but no soil

insecticide a chemical that kills insects

legume a group of plants that includes peas and beans

malnutrition bad health as a result of not eating enough food or the right kinds of food

microbes very small organisms such as bacteria

minerals substances found in foods that are essential to keep us healthy

nutrients substances in soil that make crops grow, and in foods that nourish us

pesticides chemicals that kill pests that damage crops, such as insects

protein a substance found in foods that we need to help us grow and stay healthy

reservoirs large pools of collected water

solar-powered converting energy from the sun into power

staple food a food that is a main source of nutrition for a community, such as rice or wheat

sustainable not wasting resources or causing harm to the environment

vitamins substances found in foods that are essential to keep us healthy

yields the amount of crops produced

For More Information

Books

Faulkner, Nicholas, and Janey Levy. *Conservation and You*. New York, NY: Rosen Central, 2019.

Mason, Paul. *Making Our Food Sustainable*. New York, NY: Crabtree Publishing Company, 2019.

Rooney, Anne. *Agricultural Engineering and Feeding the Future*. New York, NY: Crabtree Publishing Company, 2016.

Steele, Philip. *Analyzing the Food Supply Chain: Asking Questions, Evaluating Evidence, and Designing Solutions*. New York, NY: Cavendish Square, 2019.

Websites

Find out how fishers are protecting our oceans and seas at:
www.greenwave.org

Discover more about the ingenious innovation Pluumo at:
www.pluumo.com/home

Read up on how Thought For Food is making a difference at:
www.thoughtforfood.org

Find out more about the WWF Smart Gear Competition at:
www.worldwildlife.org/initiatives/international-smart-gear-competition

Publisher's note to educators and parents:
Our editors have carefully reviewed these websites to ensure that they are suitable for students. Many websites change frequently, however, and we cannot guarantee that a site's future contents will continue to meet our high standards of quality and educational value. Be advised that students should be closely supervised whenever they access the Internet.

Index